Sienna Searches for

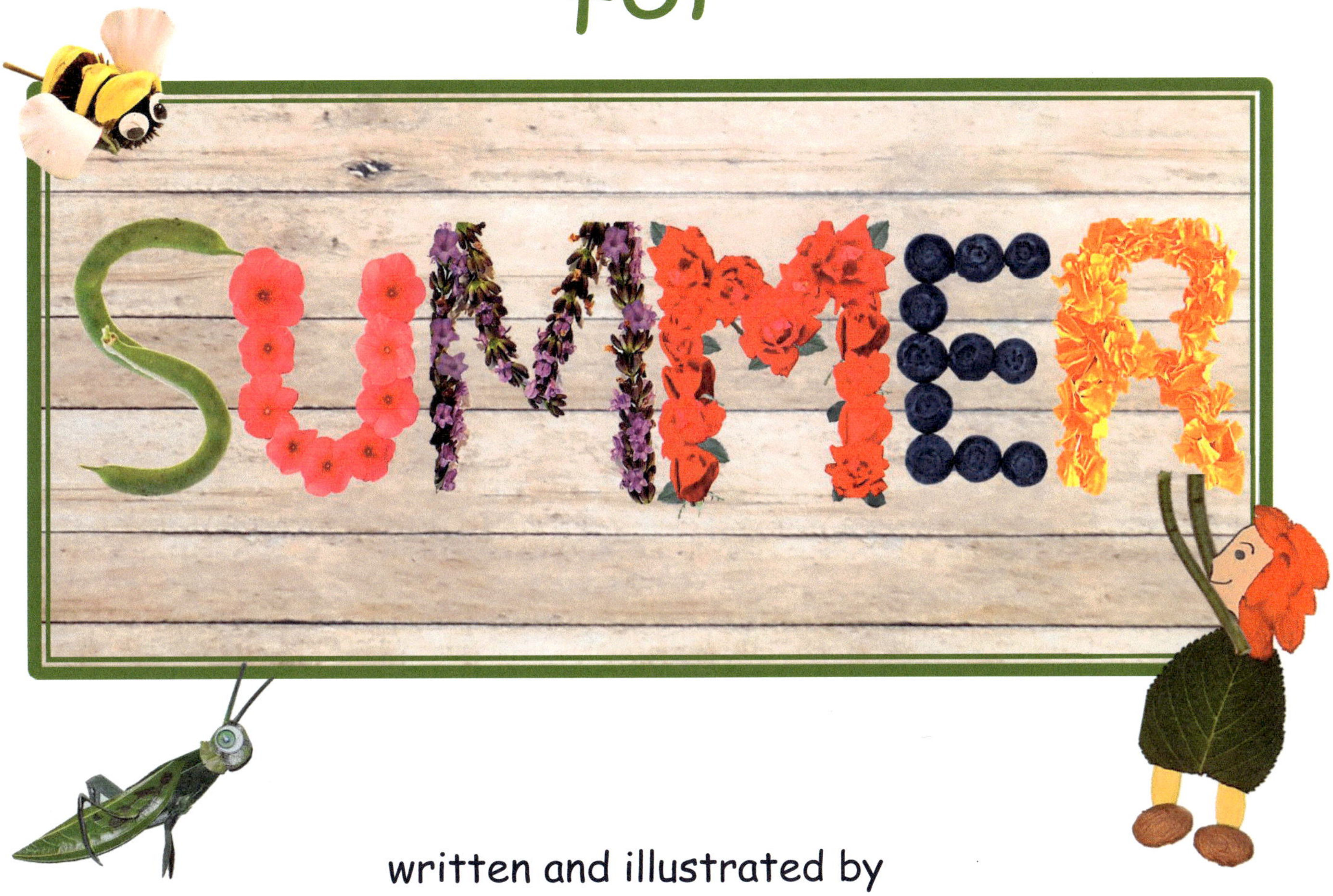

SUMMER

written and illustrated by
Colleen Driscoll

Sienna Searches for Summer

by Colleen Driscoll

Additional copies of this book are available from Amazon.com, KDP, and other retail outlets

To contact the author:

Email: cdriscollauthor@yahoo.com
www.cdriscollauthor.wixsite.com/colleendriscoll

Kindle Direct Publishing

ISBN-9798336669909

Driscoll, Colleen
Sienna Searches for Summer by Colleen Driscoll

For my garden friends

One day, Sienna collected wildflowers in her basket. She waved to her friend Silas. "Where are you going?" Sienna asked.

"I'm going to visit Flora," Silas said. "We can play all day now that summer's here."

"What is summer?" Sienna asked.

"Look around," Silas said, stretching his arms wide. "You'll find it." He waved and ran down the road.

Sienna called out to a colorful butterfly in the sky. "Will you help me search for summer?"

The butterfly fluttered her wings. "I can help you later," she said, circling around a cluster of daisies. "I have to collect nectar and pollen while the flowers are in bloom."

Sienna watched Mr. Chipmunk scurry across the grass and pick a clover blossom. "Will you help me find summer?" she asked.

Mr. Chipmunk chomped on the clover. "I'll help you after I eat," he answered and then burped. "Pardon me. There are so many tasty plants to snack on in the summer."

Soon, a lizard slithered down a tall tree onto the ground.

"Lizard, what does summer look like?" Sienna asked.

"Summer looks different depending on where you live," the dry, scaly lizard said as he stretched out to bask on his favorite rock. "Here, near the forest, summer is soaking up the hot sunrays and warming my body while I nap.

"But for my relatives who live at the beach, summer is burying in hot sand during the long days and running in salty ocean water."

Next, Sienna met Ms. Opossum who was watching her passel of joeys. "Hello, Ms. Opossum," Sienna said. "Your babies are very playful today."

Ms. Opossum laughed. "They keep me busy. Baby animals born in the spring will grow all summer and learn to take care of themselves."

"What is summer?" Sienna asked.

"Summer is many things," Ms. Opossum said.

"Summer is when plants mature to bear fruit, nuts, and seeds.

"Flowers burst into bright colors,
and tree leaves turn a deep green.

"During the summer, the sun moves across the sky giving us extra daylight. Even the sunflower spends its day following the sun's movements."

"Can you feel summer?"
Sienna wondered out loud.
Ms. Opossum nodded.
"You can feel the summer
sun heat your cheeks."

Blackberries

Strawberries

Ms. Opossum picked berries in the grass and handed some to Sienna. "You can taste summer, too. Summer is ripe berries ready for eating."

Blueberries

Raspberries

After Sienna ate the sweet berries, she picked a fuzzy peach from a tree and bit into it. "Mmmm. This is so tangy and juicy!"

Ms. Opossum smiled. "Summer is sweet, ripened fruits like peaches, plums, and watermelon."

Ms. Opossum pointed to birds singing in the trees. "Summer is baby birds peeking from their nests and fledglings learning how to fly."

Sienna tilted her head. "I hear chirping in the grass."

Ms. Opossum nodded. "Birds aren't the only singers in the summer. Buzzing bumblebees and chirping crickets and grasshoppers make music, too.

"Summer is also beetles, ladybugs, stink bugs,

fireflies, mosquitoes, and moths."

Thunder rumbled in the distance. "Oh, no!" Ms. Opossum said. "I must get home before it storms." She gathered her joeys onto her back. "Where we live summer is flashing lightning and booming thunderstorms.

"In some places summer means long, dry periods with no rain."

When Sienna reached her house,
the thunder stopped. The dark
clouds had passed, and the sun was
shining again.

Sienna stared at her garden and picked up the hose. "Too bad it didn't rain. The plants are wilting."

As she watered the vegetables, Silas and Flora walked by.

"Hi, Sienna. How did your search for summer go?" Silas asked.

"It went great," Sienna said. "Signs are everywhere. Summer is sun-ripened tomatoes, crunchy green beans, crisp carrots, and sweet corn on the cob."

Silas smiled. "Very good!"

Flora wiped the sweat from her brow. "I'd love to go swimming. I'm hot."

"I know another sign of summer," Sienna said. She pointed the hose high in the air and laughed. "Summer is the perfect time to cool down with my friends!"

Nature materials used in Sienna Searches for Summer

Sienna: orange coneflower (hair accessory) coneflower petals (hair and legs), hydrangea leaf (body), nutmeg shells (shoes), flower stems (arms)
Basket: old leaf, flowers: carnation, hydrangea, black-eyed Susan, pinecones, snapdragons
Yellow creature in basket: chrysanthemum

Silas: dandelion (hair), leaf (body), black walnut and walnut shell (shoes), stems (arms and legs)
Yellow creature peeking from basket: chrysanthemum
Background: marigolds and carnations

Sienna: coneflower petals (hair and legs), hydrangea leaf (body), nutmeg shells (shoes), flower stems (arms)
Basket: old leaf, **Flowers**: carnation, hydrangea, black-eyed Susan, pinecones, snapdragons
Yellow creature in basket: chrysanthemum
Clouds: blue hydrangeas

Large butterfly: rose petals, petunia petals, lavender (center), flower stamens (antennae)
Small butterflies: hydrangea petals
Background: daisies

Chipmunk: catkins from quaking aspen tree, pinecones petals, mosses
Background: clover blossoms in grass

Sienna: coneflower petals (hair and legs), hydrangea leaf (body), nutmeg shells (shoes), flower stems (arms)
Yellow creature in basket: chrysanthemum
Chipmunk: catkins from quaking aspen tree, pinecones petals, mosses

Tree: bark and maple leaves
Salamander: calla lily petal & yellow coneflower petal
Sienna: coneflower petals (hair and legs), hydrangea leaf (body), nutmeg shells (shoes), flower stems (arms)
Creature in basket: chrysanthemum

Sun: marigold petals
Salamander: calla lily petal & yellow coneflower petal
Background: leaves and stones

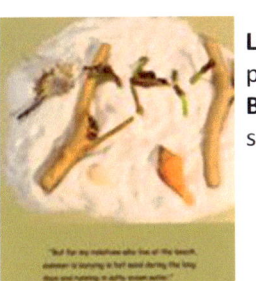

Lizard: gladiolus flower stem, pinecone petals
Background: sand, driftwood, seashells

Lizard: hydrangea leaf and pinecone petals
Background waves: hydrangea blossoms, stones, and cut sea glass; seashells

Sienna: orange coneflower (hair accessory) coneflower petals (hair and legs), hydrangea leaf (body), nutmeg shells (shoes),
Flowers in basket: carnation, hydrangea, black-eyed Susan, pinecones, snapdragons
Yellow creature in basket: chrysanthemum

Opossum: white coneflower petals, dried chrysanthemum petals, ears-black center of black-eyed Susan, pink coneflower petal (clawed feet and tongue), flower stem (tail)
Background: bark, maple leaves

Tomato plant and fruit
Sycamore plant and seed-ball

Assorted flowers: coneflowers, black-eyed Susan, zinnias, daisies, hydrangea, gladiolus, rose, snapdragon
Leaves: maple, sweetgum, quaking aspen

Bumblebee: black center of black-eyed Susan, wings vinca petals, stripes yellow chrysanthemum
Ladybug: rose petal
Sunflowers

Sun: yellow chrysanthemum petals
Sienna: orange coneflower (hair accessory) coneflower petals (hair), hydrangea leaf (body),

Opossum face: dried zinnia petals, white chrysanthemum petals, **ears**—centers of a black-eyed Susan

Ants: black-eyed Susan centers, thin twigs (legs)

Birds: chrysanthemum petals (feathers), carnation petals (head and face), coneflower petals (beak and feet)
Bird nest: abandoned bird's nest

Grasshopper: leaves, stem
Cricket: bark, acorn top, sticks
Bumblebee: black center of black-eyed Susan, wings impatiens petals, stripes yellow chrysanthemum

Stink bugs: pinecone petals, lavender (legs)
Ladybugs: rose petals
Beetles: coneflower petals, dried lavender and petals (legs)
Background: Queen Anne's lace, petunias, daylily, geranium

Fireflies: impatiens petals, cucumber blossom (yellow light);
Moths: carnation petals;
Mosquitos: chrysanthemum petals
Moon: impatiens petals

Opossum: white coneflower petals, dried chrysanthemum petals, black center of black-eyed Susan (eyes), pink coneflower petal (paws), flower stem (tail), cut lavender pieces (joeys' eyes)
Cloud & Rain: chrysanthemum petals
Lightning: chrysanthemum petals

Tall cacti: flower petals
Round cacti: cucumbers, carnations;
Tumbleweeds: Coneflower centers
Lizards: gladiolus stem, pinecone petals
Snakes: dried leaves, aloe vera leaf
Background: sand, rocks

Sun: snapdragon petals,
Garden: leaves, cucumber blossom, purple pansy (eggplant), orange coneflower petals (carrots), snapdragon petals (corn), carnation petals (tomatoes), sticks (fence)
Roof: tree bark

Sienna: coneflower petals (hair and legs), hydrangea leaf (body), nutmeg shells (shoes), flower stems (arms)
Water: gladiolus flower; Hose: flower stem; **Butterflies**: hydrangea petals
Garden: tomato plant and fruit, bean plant, blossom, and bean
Creature in basket: chrysanthemum

Silas: dandelion (hair), leaf (body), black walnut and walnut shell (shoes), stems (arms and legs)
Flora: Sycamore seed pod and Royal Purple Smokebush leaf (hat), dried seedpod (arms), Smokebush leaf (body & legs), black walnut shells (shoes)

Flora: Sycamore seed pod and Royal Purple Smokebush leaf (hat), dried seedpod (arms), Royal Purple Smokebush leaf (body & legs)
Pond water and Flora's sweat drops: Blue Delphiniums
Background: thistles, stones, boxwood leaves

Silas: dandelion (hair), leaf (body), black walnut & walnut shell (shoes), stems (arms & legs)
Flora: Sycamore seed pod and Royal Purple Smokebush leaf (hat), dried seedpod (arms), Royal Purple Smokebush leaf (body & legs), black walnut shells (shoes)
Sienna: orange coneflower (hair accessory) coneflower petals (hair and legs), hydrangea leaf (body), nutmeg shells (shoes), flower stems (arms)
Water: gladiolus flower; **Hose**: flower stem

Made in the USA
Columbia, SC
24 September 2024

42941291R00020